NATHAN WEBB

GOD
AND THE
MACHINE

NAVIGATING FAITH
IN THE AGE OF AI

ABINGDON PRESS | NASHVILLE

God and the Machine
Navigating Faith in the Age of AI
Leader Guide

978-1-7910-4108-3

Cover description: A human hand and a robotic hand reach toward each other against a soft red and beige background overlaid with faint binary code. Bold red text reads *God and the Machine* with *Leader Guide* at the top and *Navigating Faith in the Age of AI* in capital letters at the bottom.

MANUFACTURED IN
THE UNITED STATES OF AMERICA

CONTENTS

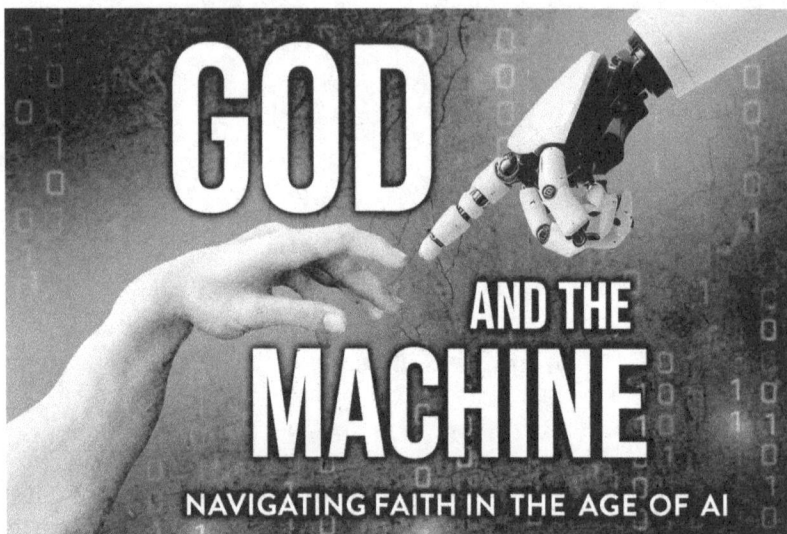

GOD
AND THE
MACHINE
NAVIGATING FAITH IN THE AGE OF AI

Enjoy a short video message from
the author for each chapter of
God and the Machine:
Navigating Faith in the Age of AI.
Great for launching small-group discussion!

Scan the QR code above or visit
https://bit.ly/godandthemachinevideos

Introduction

For many people today, artificial intelligence (AI) seems ever-present. Whether in news stories, using it at work or home, discussions about ethical implications, fears about job security, or visions of how it might reshape our society, AI seems to have rapidly become a pressing concern in many areas of life.

God and the Machine: Navigating Faith in the Age of AI takes on the topic of AI—what it is, what it does, and what kinds of questions we should be asking about its use, especially in a church context—from a distinctly Christian perspective. The author, Nathan Webb, a United Methodist minister serving a digital-first church, provides an introduction to the rapidly evolving world of AI and the ethical and theological issues it raises for all of us.

This Leader Guide is intended to help you lead a small group of adults from your congregation in a study of *God and the Machine: Navigating Faith in the Age of AI*. It gives you logistical pointers, Scripture readings, and study questions you can use to plan and lead six sessions, corresponding to the six chapters of the book. The questions are designed to be open-ended: they are not matters of right or wrong; rather, they are prompts for deeper thought and thus deeper engagement with the topic of AI and its intersection with the church, Christianity, and Christian ethics.

Session 1—What Is AI, Really?

In this chapter, AI is introduced as a practical tool with ethical and spiritual implications. We are tasked with discerning guidelines for the ethical use of technology and warned against replacing human judgment with automation. Drawing from Scripture, Nathan underscores the sacredness of human creativity and calls for disciplined, transparent, and ethical AI use in ministry and church settings, especially when it involves human relationships.

Session 2—Generated in Whose Image?

This chapter explores the theological tension between human creativity as an expression of the *imago Dei* and the growing use of artificial intelligence. Nathan notes that some of the most vociferous skepticism about AI arises from people in creative fields who sense that something important is at stake. Creativity is also rooted in God's nature as Creator, and Nathan argues that when humans create, they echo divine artistry. AI, however, cannot truly create—only reassemble and imitate. The chapter also engages in discussion of AI slop and deepfake images, which point to the dangers of pushing out human discernment and a desire for truth.

Session 3—Does God Use Technology?

This chapter contends that technology, including AI, is ethically and morally neutral but is effective only when guided by human wisdom. In ministry, AI can support tasks like worship planning, accessibility, and outreach, but human oversight is essential, especially in prayer, scriptural interpretation, and any task directly involving relationships with others. Misuse or unreflective reliance on AI or similar systems risks harm, but ethical, prayerful application can amplify God's love, inclusion, and spiritual engagement. The chapter emphasizes that the key is not whether God uses technology but how humans employ it wisely for God's purposes, prioritizing ethics, discernment, and relational care.

Session 4—The Ethics Engine

AI offers opportunity but carries ethical risks, including bias, privacy violations, and the spread of fake images and misinformation. Intuition alone is insufficient; proactive frameworks are needed to prevent prejudice and protect marginalized voices. Truth, consent, and transparency are paramount, especially when handling sensitive content. Churches are called to lead in digital literacy and ethical AI adoption, ensuring that technology serves God and neighbor rather than undermining trust, justice, and integrity. Ethics, the "engine" of AI, must guide adoption, balancing innovation with responsibility, protection, and the upholding of biblical principles.

Session 5—The Church in the Age of Machines

The author explores digital-first church planting, defining church in a tech-driven era using early church models and Wesleyan structures. The community the author pastors, Checkpoint Church, uses a variety of innovative and technological means to make possible a new kind of church community. AI supports outreach, community management, and logistics, but does not replace pastoral care and genuine human relationships. Using the Wesleyan Quadrilateral, AI's ethical and practical applications are also evaluated here, with the finding that technology can enhance but not redefine the church's mission. The chapter stresses that while digital tools extend reach and effectiveness, the church's essence remains rooted in human presence, relational connection, and spiritual practices.

Session 6—Human-Forward Thinking

This chapter examines the tension between human embodiment and AI using the metaphor of the "ghost in the machine." Digital spaces do not negate human presence; empathy, care, and relational connection are still operative online. AI should augment human work, freeing people for ethical, relational, and ecological responsibilities. Trust, transparency, and intentional engagement are essential, and the church should prioritize love, hope, and community over suspicion or technological cleverness. Christians are called to integrate AI thoughtfully while taking seriously embodied human presence. Technology, including AI, is a tool God can use, but the ultimate focus is on humans bringing Christ into both physical and digital spaces.

HOW TO USE THIS GUIDE

This guide is flexible. You may want to follow the format precisely and thus offer informative background as well as raise questions for fruitful reflection and decisions. You may also adapt it to your preferred method of group facilitation as well as add information that you have found through research you did to prepare for this study. Choose the questions and activities that you find most appropriate for your group. You may find that each group, even if from the same church, will benefit from a different set of activities or questions.

Each session plan in this Leader Guide contains the following:

- **Session Goals** to help you focus on outcomes most relevant and helpful to your group.
- **Biblical Foundations** are the main Scripture texts in each session. Some of these will be longer excerpts from passages highlighted in *God and the Machine*, while others are not explicitly discussed but relate to the themes of the book. The

passages are taken from the New Revised Standard Version (Updated Edition) without verse numbers to support reading each passage as a whole unit.

+ **Before Your Session** to help make basic preparations.
+ **Starting Your Session** contains ideas for icebreaker conversations and/or activities related to the readings to help engage people in the class.
+ **Discussion Questions** are provided as suggestions only. You will likely not have time to use all questions provided. Use the ones that seem appropriate to you to guide and shape a lively, constructive discussion. You may want to create your own questions or tell the participants to contact you during the week in case they have additional questions they want to discuss.
+ **Opening and Closing Prayers** are included for each week. Please feel free to adapt these prayers for the needs of your group or substitute your own.

PLANNING AND CONDUCTING THE SESSIONS

Planning Tips

+ **Subject matter.** If you are unfamiliar with AI and how it works, you may want to seek out some reputable sources to familiarize yourself with this new technology. You may also want to experiment with an AI like ChatGPT or Claude if you have not done so before. Although God and the Machine is intended for people with all levels of experience with AI and does not engage deeply with the technical details of these systems, it is important to understand the basics of how this technology works in order to understand its limitations and the ethical quandaries it raises.

- **Group size.** This study works best when it is used in gatherings that are not too large. A group of six to twelve people may be optimal, as it allows time for all to share their thoughts. If a number of people are interested in participating—which is a positive development—start more than one group, and train more than one person to lead the groups.

- **Length of sessions.** A meeting of once a week is usually optimal; we suggest around sixty minutes of meeting time.

- **Location.** You might choose a central location where participants are used to gathering, such as the church building, or in a participant or leader's home, if that is preferable. You might also consider using an online meeting platform. Whatever the meeting site or format, the location should be quiet, free of interruption from family members and pets, and private, for the sake of confidentiality.

Before Each Meeting

- **Familiarize yourself with the content.** Read the book chapter, the Bible verses, and the week's session plan. Take your time with the Scripture reading, paying attention to aspects of the text you have not noticed before.

- **Read through the Leader Guide section for the week and determine which of the suggested activities and discussion questions you will use.** Think about which are most appropriate for your group and make those a priority. Be sure to ask your group what activities they are finding most helpful. Be prepared to adjust the session as group members interact and questions arise.

- **Think ahead about how you might respond to the questions.** Sometimes, if group members are hesitant, you may want to offer some response to a question or give ideas about possible responses. You do not have to provide definitive answers to the questions. The questions are designed to prompt imagination, reflection, exploration, and sharing.

+ **Four to two weeks before the first meeting, help participants obtain the main book, *God and the Machine* by Nathan Webb.** Consider buying copies of the book to distribute them in advance of the class. You may also send links to Cokesbury .com so participants can buy the book on their own. Ask them to read the book's introduction and chapter 1 in advance. The introduction is important, as it sets the foundation for the book.

SESSION 1

What Is AI, Really?

SESSION GOALS

This session's reading, reflection, discussion, and prayer will help participants:

+ Gain a more precise, realistic, and nuanced understanding of what AI (artificial intelligence) is, how it works, and what its uses and capabilities are.
+ Dispel misconceptions about AI and both its potential benefits and dangers.
+ Understand AI as a tool that can be used for many purposes.
+ Understand the need for a Christian ethic that thinks critically about AI and the complexities around its use.

BIBLICAL FOUNDATIONS

When the Pharisees heard that he had silenced the Sadducees, they gathered together, and one of them, an expert in the law, asked him a question to test him. "Teacher, which commandment in the law is the greatest?" He said to him, "'You shall love the Lord your God with all your heart and with all your soul and with all your mind.' This is the greatest and first commandment. And a second is like it: 'You shall love your neighbor as yourself.' On these two commandments hang all the Law and the Prophets."

(Matthew 22:34-40)

"I have said these things to you while I am still with you. But the Advocate, the Holy Spirit, whom the Father will send in my name, will teach you everything and remind you of all that I have said to you. Peace I leave with you; my peace I give to you. I do not give to you as the world gives. Do not let your hearts be troubled, and do not let them be afraid."

(John 14:25-27)

BEFORE YOUR SESSION

+ Carefully and prayerfully read this session's Biblical Foundations. Note words and phrases that attract your attention and think about them. Why did you find them of interest? Did they surprise you? Confuse you? Write down questions you have and try to answer them. You may want to consult trusted Bible commentaries.
+ Carefully read chapter 1 of *God and the Machine*.
+ You will need Bibles for in-person participants and/or screen slides prepared with Scripture texts for sharing (identify the translation used); for note-taking and brainstorming, you may want to have newsprint or a markerboard and markers; paper, pens or pencils.

STARTING YOUR SESSION

Welcome participants. Talk briefly about why you are excited to lead this study of *God and the Machine* by Nathan Webb and what you hope to gain from it. Invite volunteers to talk about why they are interested in this study and their hopes for it.

It may be helpful to have participants share and discuss their level of experience with and knowledge of AI. This may open avenues for further questions and discussion as well as give participants and leaders a sense of the group's familiarity with AI. Consider asking participants to share about the following questions:

+ Who here has used AI before? (perhaps ChatGPT, Claude, AI Mode in Google, or the AI Overview that appears at the top of Google searches) What have you used it for? Work? Creative pursuits? Internet searching? Data analysis?
+ What has your experience of using AI been? What positives and negatives about the technology have you noticed?
+ Whether you have used it or not, what are your general feelings about AI? What images and ideas does it bring up for you?

OPENING PRAYER

God, as we learn about the technologies shaping our world today, grant us curiosity without fear and wisdom without pride. Help guide our words and thoughts as we seek to understand the rapid changes these technologies have brought. And help us wrestle with the questions and dilemmas they have created. We ask for the courage to face our unknown future with the peace of Christ ruling in our hearts. Amen.

WHAT IS AI, REALLY?

Discuss:

+ Nathan Webb, the author of *God and the Machine*, states "Technology is what knowledge looks like with it's applied to achieving a goal." Do you find this a useful way to think about this topic?

+ How might this definition change the way you think about your phone, your car, or even a church live stream?

+ When you hear the word *artificial*, what assumptions come with it? How does it contrast with words like *creative* or *spiritual*?

+ The author distinguishes predictive AI (which anticipates) from generative AI (which creates). What are examples of each kind of AI?

+ As Nathan points out, current AI technologies rely on massive amounts of data, text, and images for training. This has become a controversial issue, since not all the authors or creators of this media consent to their work being used for AI training. How do you feel about this issue? Should there be limits on what AI training consists of?

+ How do you think the line between human and machine creativity might blur—and does that concern or inspire you? Why?

FEARS IN A TECHNOLOGICAL AGE

Discuss:

+ The author notes that fear has accompanied almost every new technology—from the printing press to credit cards. Over the years, what technologies can you recall seeing or experiencing fear about? What kinds of fears about AI do you hear in the church or media today?

+ In what ways can fear be protective? What possible advantages or good reasons are there for being fearful? On the other hand, when does it become spiritually harmful?

+ Jesus tells us not to let our hearts be troubled or afraid. How might that peace look when we talk about machines that seem to "think"?

+ What practices, whether spiritual, communal, or intellectual, help you stay grounded when the world feels uncertain or moving too fast?

THE DIVINE IMAGE, ETHICS, AND TRANSPARENCY

Discuss:

+ What does it mean that humans are made in the image of God? How does this shape our creativity? (Note that this topic will be discussed further in the next session.)

+ Nathan insists that AI does *not* bear God's image. What does this mean, and why does it matter?

+ What are the dangers of treating an AI, or other form of technology, as human?

+ In your own life, where do you see technology helping you fulfill your vocation as a steward of creation? Where does it tempt you to neglect that role?

+ The author points out that algorithms are designed to keep us engaged for corporate profit. What moral or spiritual questions does that raise for Christians?

+ How can we practice truth-telling and transparency in our own digital lives?

+ The author calls for churches to "start with transparency." What does that look like in worship, communications, and teaching?

+ Have you ever experienced a time when technology distorted your perception of truth or relationships? How might faith communities help people resist such distortions?

- What parallels can you see between discernment in theology and discernment in technology—between interpreting Scripture and wrestling with the advent of new technologies?

MISSION IN A DIGITAL WORLD

Discuss:

- The author argues that "all nations" in the Great Commission may now include digital spaces and online communities. Do you agree with this way of seeing things? What would this mean in practice? What new possibilities might this idea open up for the church?
- How might using AI for accessibility (for example, captioning, translation, or adaptive technology) reflect the inclusive spirit of the Great Commission and Jesus's teachings?
- In what ways can we ensure that technology supports genuine relationship and discipleship rather than replacing them with something else entirely?

FAITHFUL RESPONSES TO ARTIFICIAL INTELLIGENCE

Draw the group's attention back to the author's conclusion: "AI isn't evil. It's not alive. It's not demonic. It's a tool. But like any tool, it needs ethical guidance." Discuss:

- Do you agree with this general sentiment? Why or why not?
- How does that statement challenge popular fears or fantasies about AI?

+ What theological criteria could help you decide whether a use of technology is "beneficial," to borrow Paul's language from 1 Corinthians 10:23?
+ How might transparency about AI use build trust in a congregation? What would transparency look like?
+ The author says we must "find God within" AI and put it to good use. What do you think that means? Where have you glimpsed God at work in your own uses of technology?

CLOSING YOUR SESSION

Have participants write down and/or share aloud about the following question.

+ What are the important open questions you see about AI and technology use today? What about specifically in church contexts?

Time permitting, you may want to engage in some discussion on these questions. They may also guide what you focus on with the group in subsequent sessions. If participants raise questions about how the technology works or other factual matters, group members may offer answers or resources for study.

CLOSING PRAYER

God of wisdom and truth, you have given us minds to think, hearts to feel, and hands to create. We thank you for every discovery that expands human understanding, even those that unsettle us, causing us to question what we once held as true. Keep us mindful that nothing can replace your presence with us and our presence with each other. Teach us to use our tools in ways that build up love, justice, compassion, and peace for the purposes of your kingdom. Through Jesus Christ, Amen.

SESSION 2

Generated in Whose Image?

SESSION GOALS

This session's reading, reflection, discussion, and prayer will help participants:

+ Reflect on the meaning of the *imago Dei*, especially as it relates to human creativity.
+ Think critically about the differences between human creation and machine-generated images and text.
+ Examine how AI affects creativity, faith, and Christian witness.
+ Consider the ethical responsibilities involved with using AI technology.
+ Explore how to respond faithfully to AI's role in art, ministry, and communication.

BIBLICAL FOUNDATIONS

And God said, "Let the earth bring forth living creatures of every kind: cattle and creeping things and wild animals of the earth of every kind."

GOD AND THE MACHINE: LEADER GUIDE

And it was so. God made the wild animals of the earth of every kind and the cattle of every kind and everything that creeps upon the ground of every kind. And God saw that it was good.

Then God said, "Let us make humans in our image, according to our likeness, and let them have dominion over the fish of the sea and over the birds of the air and over the cattle and over all the wild animals of the earth and over every creeping thing that creeps upon the earth.

>*So God created humans in his image,*
>>*in the image of God he created them;*
>>*male and female he created them.*

God blessed them, and God said to them, "Be fruitful and multiply and fill the earth and subdue it and have dominion over the fish of the sea and over the birds of the air and over every living thing that moves upon the earth."

(Genesis 1:24-28)

The LORD spoke to Moses, "See, I have called by name Bezalel son of Uri son of Hur, of the tribe of Judah and I have filled him with a divine spirit, with ability, intelligence, and knowledge, and every kind of skill, to devise artistic designs, to work in gold, silver, and bronze, in cutting stones for setting, and in carving wood, to work in every kind of craft. Moreover, I have appointed with him Oholiab son of Ahisamach, of the tribe of Dan, and I have given skill to all the skillful, so that they may make all that I have commanded you: the tent of meeting, and the ark of the covenant, and the cover that is on it, and all the furnishings of the tent, the table and its utensils, and the pure lampstand with all its utensils, and the altar of incense, and the altar of burnt offering with all its utensils, and the basin with its stand, and the finely worked vestments, the holy vestments for the priest Aaron and the vestments of his sons, for their service as priests, and the anointing oil and the fragrant incense for the holy place. They shall do just as I have commanded you."

(Exodus 31:1-11)

BEFORE YOUR SESSION

+ Carefully and prayerfully read this session's Biblical Foundations. Note words and phrases that attract your attention and think about them. Why did you find them of interest? Did they surprise you? Confuse you? Write down questions you have and try to answer them. You may want to consult trusted Bible commentaries.
+ Carefully read chapter 2 of *God and the Machine*.
+ You will need Bibles for in-person participants and/or screen slides prepared with Scripture texts for sharing (identify the translation used); for note-taking and brainstorming, you may want to have newsprint or a markerboard and markers; paper, pens or pencils.

STARTING YOUR SESSION

Welcome participants and ask them if they had any reflections about last week's session. You may want to review some of the thoughts that people shared, especially if you find that they relate to chapter 2.

Art and creativity are key topics in this chapter and in discussions of AI more generally. It may be helpful here for participants to reflect on their own creative activities and processes. Discuss:

+ What creative pursuits do you enjoy? This could be many things: writing, photography, painting, knitting, cooking, acting, gardening, flower arranging, music, singing, church choir, and so on.
+ What is your creative process? How do you encourage and sustain your creativity?

+ Do you use technology at all in your creative pursuits? How?
+ Optional: Show examples of AI-generated art and ask for first impressions. You can use some of the AI programs mentioned in the book or conduct an internet search for AI art with some additional search times (like "AI art Jesus" or "AI art landscape," for example).

OPENING PRAYER

God, Creator of the universe, you formed us in your image and invited us to share in the joy of creating. We thank you for all our diverse gifts and the ability and freedom to use them to express ourselves and bring joy to others. Grant us wisdom and understanding as we consider how technology can be ethically and faithfully used in ways that magnify your name and preserve your image in us. Amen.

WE WERE CREATED TO CREATE

+ Why do you think creative professionals tend to express the loudest concerns about AI?
+ Nathan centers his discussion of the *imago Dei* on creativity. Why does he do this? What other possibilities are there for how we bear the image of God?
+ In what ways do you see creativity as something that is potentially sacred or holy?
+ What does it mean to say, "We were created to create"? How does this influence how we view our work, whether artistic or otherwise?
+ What fears or hesitations do you personally feel about AI and creativity?

- Why does Nathan claim that AI-generated images are not real creative acts? What is the distinction between these images and human-generated ones? What separates real creativity from apparent creativity?

- The chapter mentions past controversies—like digital animation, synthesizers, or video games as "not real art." Do these past moments mirror today's AI debates? Why or why not?

- What does it mean to you for art to feel or be "authentic"?

- How does the involvement of AI in the creative process change (or not change) the value of the final product? Do you believe there is a basic difference between human and AI art, no matter its quality and subject matter?

- Do you agree with the author's hesitation over AI image generation? Why or why not?

- How do tools shape the meaning of art? Where do you draw the line between tools that assist creation and tools that replace it or do the creative work for you?

- How might Christians engage technology in artistic spaces without losing sight of their creative identity?

THE RESULT OF UNCHECKED ARTIFICIAL INTELLIGENCE

- Have you come across examples of AI slop online? What clued you in that it was AI? Have you ever mistaken an AI image for a real one?

- Why do you think religious imagery, like depictions of Jesus, is so easily and often co-opted by these automated systems? How might this cheapen or distort religious messages?

+ What responsibilities do Christians and faith communities have in responding to this kind of manipulation?

+ The author warns against automating ministry without oversight. Where do you see that temptation in your own community?

+ How can churches maintain genuine relational ministry in an automated world?

+ How does Paul's warning that "'All things are permitted,' but not all things are beneficial" (1 Corinthians 10:23) apply to the use of AI in ministry?

+ How might a lack of discernment in the use of AI unintentionally harm others? What are the possible negative consequences?

+ How can faith communities ensure that their AI practices align with the call to love God and neighbor? What safeguards might help us use AI while being oriented toward love and effective discipleship rather than simply convenience?

A BETTER PATH FORWARD

+ What does the story of Bezalel in Exodus 31 have to say about AI, its uses, and the pursuit of excellence? How might Bezalel's calling inspire our approach to creative and technological work today?

+ What dangers might arise when churches or creatives rely on AI to "cut corners" or otherwise prioritize efficiency?

+ Do you ever feel similar tensions or temptations in your work (both within the church and outside it)—the potential conflict between excellence (or effectiveness) and efficiency? How do we balance the need for rest and capacity with the call to give God our best?

- How can AI be used *without* sacrificing excellence?
- The chapter suggests building AI policies in churches. What values or guardrails would you include in such a policy?
- How can we call out AI misuse (like slop) with both truth and grace?
- What does it look like to hold ourselves accountable for our own online activity, especially as it relates to AI and its potential misuse?
- How might AI be used in ways that reflect God's image rather than distort it?
- What one practical step could your group or church take this year to approach AI more thoughtfully?

CLOSING YOUR SESSION

Invite each participant to identify (either with the group or to themselves) one specific way they can reflect God's image this week. This can include creative pursuits, online activity, and also the words and actions we present to others.

CLOSING PRAYER

God, maker of all things, you formed us in your image as beings infused with your creative spark. Be with us as we bring this creativity into the world, glorifying your name with each work we produce. Help us to be ever faithful to your desires for us, and show us opportunities to use our God-given abilities for the building up of the church and your kingdom. Amen.

SESSION 3

Does God Use Technology?

SESSION GOALS

This session's reading, reflection, discussion, and prayer will help participants:

- Reflect on their experiences of how people (and not tools alone) drive technological change in churches and communities.
- Explore the biblical and theological precedents for using technology wisely to advance God's mission.
- Consider how AI can be used ethically for ministry and worship.
- Develop practical frameworks for discerning when and how to use AI in their own faith communities and spiritual practices.

BIBLICAL FOUNDATIONS

"All things are permitted," but not all things are beneficial. "All things are permitted," but not all things build up. Do not seek your own advantage but that of the other. Eat whatever is sold in the meat market without

raising any question on the ground of conscience, for "the earth and its fullness are the Lord's." If an unbeliever invites you to a meal and you are disposed to go, eat whatever is set before you without raising any question on the ground of conscience. But if someone says to you, "This has been offered in sacrifice," then do not eat it, out of consideration for the one who informed you and for the sake of conscience—I mean the other's conscience, not your own. For why should my freedom be subject to the judgment of someone else's conscience? If I partake with thankfulness, why should I be denounced because of that for which I give thanks?

So, whether you eat or drink or whatever you do, do everything for the glory of God. Give no offense to Jews or to Greeks or to the church of God, just as I try to please everyone in everything I do, not seeking my own advantage but that of many, so that they may be saved.

(1 Corinthians 10:23-33)

Do you not know that, if you present yourselves to anyone as obedient slaves, you are slaves of the one whom you obey, either of sin, which leads to death, or of obedience, which leads to righteousness? But thanks be to God that you who were slaves of sin have become obedient from the heart to the form of teaching to which you were entrusted and that you, having been set free from sin, have become enslaved to righteousness. I am speaking in human terms because of your limitations. For just as you once presented your members as slaves to impurity and lawlessness, leading to even more lawlessness, so now present your members as slaves to righteousness, leading to sanctification.

(Romans 6:16-19)

BEFORE YOUR SESSION

+ Carefully and prayerfully read this session's Biblical Foundations. Note words and phrases that attract your attention and think about them. Why did you find them of interest? Did they surprise you? Confuse you? Write down questions you have and try to answer them. You may want to consult trusted Bible commentaries.

+ Carefully read chapter 3 of *God and the Machine*.

+ You will need Bibles for in-person participants and/or screen slides prepared with Scripture texts for sharing (identify the translation used); for note-taking and brainstorming, you may want to have newsprint or a markerboard and markers; paper, pens or pencils.

STARTING YOUR SESSION

Welcome participants and ask them if they had any reflections about last week's session. You may want to review some of the thoughts that people shared, especially if you find that they relate to chapter 3.

Begin by thinking together about the benefits and drawbacks that different technologies have brought into our lives. Provide the following prompts (with the blank spaces to be filled in with an existing or possible technology) and ask for volunteers to share answers:

+ Sometimes, I wish _____ was never invented because . . .

+ Sometimes, I wish _____ were real because . . .

OPENING PRAYER

God of all creation, we thank you for giving us minds to think, hands to build, and hearts to serve. Grant us insight to understand how best to use the tools we have in ways that truly support your work in the world and allow us to live up to the teachings of our Lord, Jesus Christ. And help guide us to always be your church—a community of righteousness, love, and acceptance—in all that we do. Amen.

TECHNOLOGY NEEDS A DRIVER

Discuss:

+ What is Nathan's main point in claiming that "technology needs a driver"? What does he mean by this?
+ The author states: "Is the tool holy? That's not the question. It's just a tool; it's neutral. Can the tool be useful for spreading God's love? Now we're on the right track." What does he mean by this? Do you agree with the idea here that all tools are neutral?

ARTIFICIAL INTELLIGENCE CAN BE USED FOR GOOD

Discuss:

+ Nathan names three things he does when using AI: (1) he provides good information on his end, (2) he lays a framework of expectations, and (3) he holds full control of the tool. Why is each of these important?
+ He also refers to a mentor's saying: "It is not garbage in, garbage out. It is garbage in, garbage stays." What does this mean? How does it apply to AI?
+ Nathan gives an example of using AI for helping with SEO (search engine optimization) and other tasks related to posting videos of church services. Do you agree that this is likely an ethical use of AI? What other ways can you think of that AI could be incorporated into some of the tasks at your church?

A CHRISTIAN APPEAL
TO DISCERNMENT

Discuss:

+ Nathan distinguishes between tasks he will and will not use AI for. He will not allow AI to write his sermons but will allow it to help with SEO. What is his reasoning here? Do you agree with this type of guideline?

+ Nathan writes, "If I'm uncomfortable telling people who might ask about my AI use, that might be an indication I shouldn't be using it in the ways I am." Have you ever employed a rule like this in your work or personal life? Is this a useful test for whether a particular use of technology is appropriate?

+ How would you feel about AI being involved in worship planning at your church? Do you have any reservations? What elements of worship should be protected from AI involvement?

+ The author uses the metaphor of a sewing machine versus hand stitching versus factory production. He suggests AI is more like going from needles to a sewing machine—it augments rather than replaces creative work. Do you find this analogy helpful? Why or why not?

+ Nathan discusses AI's potential for increasing accessibility in worship through captions, translation, and personalized Christian education. Which of these applications excites you most? What concerns do you have?

+ On the subject of prayer, Nathan raises the question of whether AI could augment practices like the Daily Examen. Some people have also found it helpful to ask AI models for advice with relationships, family, and other common issues. Have you ever considered using AI in this way? What do you think of it? What do you make of Nathan's comment that AI "can be a tool that helps draw that groan out of the Spirit within and around us, making our experience of prayer deeper and more effective."

WHEN AI BECOMES SIN

Discuss:

+ In this chapter, Nathan defines sin as separation from God and notes that sin is "an enslaved condition to non-righteousness, the opposite of righteousness—in other words, separation from God." What do you make of this definition? Is it helpful or illuminating in any way? Does this definition help you think about misuse of AI?

+ Nathan raises concerns about using AI to summarize personal beliefs, current events opinions, or theological positions without careful oversight. Why might these be particularly risky uses of AI?

+ This chapter emphasizes that AI is not inherently sinful, nor should its use be shameful, but careful discernment is still required. How do we balance openness to AI's benefits with vigilance about its misuse? What ideas do you have about even what kinds of concerns are most important here?

A PLAN FOR WISE USE OF ARTIFICIAL INTELLIGENCE

Review how in this chapter the author proposes a framework of four sets of questions for evaluating any technology implementation in worship. Have volunteers read aloud the four questions Nathan presents:

1. How does this technology shift the encounter? Will this deepen people's experience of God?
2. Are we using technology to create a more equitable and just space? Are we centering our accessibility efforts around the marginalized? Are we simply amplifying the comfortable?
3. Are we honoring the exceptional craft set before us? Are we creating something beautiful that honors the excellence of God, like Bezalel with the tabernacle? Or are we just creating slop?
4. Are we resisting harmful practices and consumerism?

Discuss:

+ Apply the four questions to a technology your church currently uses (projectors, sound systems, online streaming, etc.). How does it fare in this framework?
+ Work through each question together, thinking about AI use in particular.
+ Are there any questions or concerns you would add to this list, concerns or issues that you feel are not sufficiently captured?
+ Nathan writes, "No matter how cool the technology or how seamless of an experience can be made, the centerpieces of worship must be relational, empathetic, and justice-oriented, embodying presence and peace." What does this mean practically? Can you think of technologies that fail this test?
+ Nathan also mentions he has "dropped many implementations of technology that don't pass muster." What might lead a church to abandon a technology even after significant investment? Has your church had to do this or have you had to in your home or work life?

CONNECTING TO OUR LIVES TODAY

Discuss:

+ Nathan writes: "We aren't called to baptize gadgets, but we are called to be wise craftspeople like Bezalel." What is the difference between accepting a technology because it's new or impressive versus discerning whether it serves God's mission? What are the risks and potential benefits of quick adoption and discernment?

+ The chapter concludes with this: "It's not about whether God uses technology; it's about how we use technology for God." What might shift in our thinking when we consider things from this angle?

+ What technologies in your own faith practice or church community need to be evaluated through the framework noted above? Are there any that might not be serving God's mission as well as you assumed?

+ How does this book's emphasis on human responsibility and discernment change your thinking about AI compared to how you thought about it before reading this chapter or encountering this book?

CLOSING YOUR SESSION

Ask participants to think about their own use of technology and what limitations they put on it. Discuss:

+ Do you or your family have any rules or guidelines about how you use technology? What are they and how or why did they develop?

+ How do these rules or guidelines map onto the criteria and questions Nathan raises in this book, for example, the two greatest commandments and the list of four sets of questions discussed in this chapter?

+ Examples might include limits on how long you or others can use social media or games, not looking at screens a certain time before bed, not allowing or discouraging the use of cell phone or other devices during meal times, content blockers or other safety features for minors, and anything else that prescribes how and when you use technology or what you use it for at different times.

CLOSING PRAYER

God, we pray that our minds and bodies may be put to the work you have set out for us in this world. May we continue to strive to be mindful, loving, and creative craftspeople who can navigate new difficulties, circumstances, and technologies with wisdom. Help us each day to remember the teachings of Jesus to love God and neighbor while fulfilling his commission to make disciples across the earth. May our churches and our individual actions be an example to the world of the love and grace you have shown us. Amen.

SESSION 4

The Ethics Engine

SESSION GOALS

This session's reading, reflection, discussion, and prayer will help participants:

+ Understand the critical importance of ethics in the development and implementation of AI, recognizing the importance of ethical frameworks and discernment.

+ Explore the inherent biases and potential prejudices embedded in AI systems and develop strategies for mitigating them.

+ Consider the privacy concerns around AI in ministry and other contexts and establish clear boundaries around pastoral care and personal data.

+ Recognize the dangers of deepfakes and misinformation and understand the importance of authenticity, truth-telling, and media literacy.

BIBLICAL FOUNDATIONS

Has not God chosen the poor in the world to be rich in faith and to be heirs of the kingdom that he has promised to those who love him? But you have dishonored the poor person. Is it not the rich who oppress you? Is it not they who drag you into the courts? Is it not they who blaspheme the excellent name that was invoked over you?

If you really fulfill the royal law according to the scripture, "You shall love your neighbor as yourself," you do well. But if you show partiality, you commit sin and are convicted by the law as transgressors. For whoever keeps the whole law but fails in one point has become accountable for all of it. For the one who said, "You shall not commit adultery," also said, "You shall not murder." Now if you do not commit adultery but you murder, you have become a transgressor of the law. So speak and so act as those who are to be judged by the law of liberty. For judgment will be without mercy to anyone who has shown no mercy; mercy triumphs over judgment.

(*James 2:5-13*)

My brothers and sisters, if anyone is detected in a transgression, you who have received the Spirit should restore such a one in a spirit of gentleness. Take care that you yourselves are not tempted. Bear one another's burdens, and in this way you will fulfill the law of Christ. For if those who are nothing think they are something, they deceive themselves. All must test their own work; then that work, rather than their neighbor's work, will become a cause for pride. For all must carry their own loads.

Those who are taught the word must share in all good things with their teacher.

Do not be deceived; God is not mocked, for you reap whatever you sow. If you sow to your own flesh, you will reap corruption from the flesh, but if you sow to the Spirit, you will reap eternal life from the Spirit. So let us not grow weary in doing what is right, for we will reap at harvest time, if we do not give up. So then, whenever we have an opportunity, let us work for the good of all and especially for those of the family of faith.

(*Galatians 6:1-10*)

BEFORE YOUR SESSION

+ Carefully and prayerfully read this session's Biblical Foundations. Note words and phrases that attract your attention and think about them. Why did you find them of interest? Did they surprise you? Confuse you? Write down questions you have and try to answer them. You may want to consult trusted Bible commentaries.

+ Carefully read chapter 4 of *God and the Machine*.

+ You will need Bibles for in-person participants and/or screen slides prepared with Scripture texts for sharing (identify the translation used); for note-taking and brainstorming, you may want to have newsprint or a markerboard and markers; paper, pens or pencils.

STARTING YOUR SESSION

This chapter discusses how scams, deepfakes, privacy concerns, and misinformation relate to AI. Welcome participants, and ask them to share about the following:

+ Have you or someone you know ever encountered something online or elsewhere that seemed real but turned out to be false or manipulated?

+ Have you or someone you know ever been the victim of a scam or identity theft?

+ How did these events make you feel, and did they change your outlook on security, technology, or trust in others?

OPENING PRAYER

God, you are the God of truth, of uprightness, of integrity, and of authenticity. We pray that you may help us as your people to be ever more like Christ—to follow your law of righteousness and love in all areas of our lives. Grant us the strength and courage to listen to your word and put it into practice, so that we may follow our consciences and not simply the surrounding culture, with all its pressures and stresses. We hope, like your Son, to do what is right no matter the cost. Amen.

BUILDING THE ETHICS ENGINE

Discuss:

+ What does Nathan mean when he says the "check engine light is blaring" for AI but we aren't pulling over or driving to get the problem diagnosed? Do you agree with this framing of the issue?

+ He opens this section by discussing Justice Potter Stewart's famous phrase about obscenity: "I know it when I see it." Nathan argues that in the AI age, we cannot rely on our intuition alone to spot problems. What clues you into the fact that something you may be reading, hearing, or seeing has been altered, faked, or made in bad faith?

+ Nathan writes, "Ethics isn't optional. If AI is the car, then ethics should be the engine giving it the power it needs to move." What difference does it make to position ethics in this way, as an engine, as opposed to, say, a brake pedal or warning light?

+ The chapter opens with a story about AI-generated bunnies on a trampoline that fooled millions. Why does the author use this seemingly lighthearted example to introduce a serious discussion about ethics?

+ Nathan calls on churches to "lead the charge" in demanding transparency and authenticity. Why does he believe the church should take this leadership role? Do you think it is equipped to do this well? What would it look like for the church to act in this way?

DIAGNOSING THE CHECK ENGINE LIGHT

Discuss:

+ This section distinguishes between bias and prejudice. Bias is a "disproportionate inclination for or against something," while prejudice is a "preconceived notion built without sufficient reason." Why is this distinction important for understanding AI?

+ Nathan mentions an example of misgendering someone named Logan. How might AI's biases manifest in different contexts—medical, financial, criminal justice, or ministry settings? What various uses of AI can you think of where such biases might become real problems?

+ The author discusses the example of how an image generator might create a white Jesus instead of one reflecting someone from Nazareth. What does this reveal about the data sets used in AI training?

+ Consider the AI Grok and the removal of its safety guardrails, leading to offensive and anti-Semitic responses. What do you make of this example? Is it a meaningful warning or an outlier? What does this suggest about the relationship between developer choices and AI behavior?

+ How does the biblical prohibition against partiality in James 2 (quoted in the participant book and at greater length in the Biblical Foundations above) apply to our use of AI in churches?

+ What does the author mean when he says we should *"start with the assumption that the AI is biased"* and "Everything should be double-checked, every time"? If you use AI, do you follow this guideline?

+ In this section, Nathan describes building justice-oriented directives into his AI's memory, including John Wesley's General Rules of "doing no harm" and "doing good." What would this look like in practice? What such directives would you want to build into an AI system in different contexts?

+ Nathan emphasizes that we can control what AI takes in as data. What are the practical steps he recommends? How might churches or individuals implement these strategies?

+ The book cites the film *Her* and services like Character.ai as examples of people forming emotional attachments to AI. (Notably, the film *Her* is not dark and dystopian, nor is it overtly a warning against such emotional attachments). Should we be concerned about these kind of attachments? Do they say something about our society? What are their potential benefits?

LESSONS FROM DIGITAL CHURCH

Discuss:

+ This section notes that AI often exhibits more empathy than humans in virtual conversations, but this empathy is simulated, not genuine. Does this distinction matter? Why?

+ Nathan states that AI "is not capable of . . . emotional discernment" and cannot "create a long-term trust-based relationship." Do you agree with these statements? What implications do these ideas have for therapy and pastoral care?

+ The author states, "I believe we should abstain from any incorporation of artificial intelligence into emotional reasoning or pastoral care. AI should not be used to gather prayer requests or to attend upon them." Do you agree with this boundary? Why or why not? Are there any exceptions?

+ In this chapter, the author mentions not allowing AI to have access to pastoral care conversations or other sensitive data. What boundaries should churches (or individuals) adopt around data like this?

+ What does adopting a framework of radical transparency around data mean and why might it be important? How would it be applied in a church context?

+ The author discusses some personal boundaries around reading Discord messages related to his church, saying that while Discord users consent to posting in a public server, they may not expect the pastor to read every message. What do you make of this? Does this difference between technical consent and practical expectation matter in this case?

THE SCARIEST CONSEQUENCE OF AI

Discuss:

+ Nathan describes a hypothetical scenario in which a deepfake video claiming to be from him solicits money for cryptocurrency or orphan support. How realistic is this scenario? Have you or your church encountered similar scams?

+ In this section, the author addresses his own fear about deepfakes and their potential for harm but generally cautions against fear-based responses. What is the distinction here and why might it be important?

+ Nathan connects deepfakes to the ninth commandment: "You shall not bear false witness against your neighbor" (Exodus 20:16). How does this commandment apply to deepfakes and other AI-generated misinformation? How does this commandment influence your online behavior in general?

+ In this section, there is mention of a Twitch streamer who created an AI Jesus and expresses concern about virtual avatars trained on John Wesley's writings. Are these creations potentially problematic or dangerous? Why or why not?

+ "We shouldn't assume to speak for Jesus," claims Nathan. What does he mean here in relation to AI and deepfake content? In what other ways *do* we or others speak for Jesus? How is this different from, or similar to, the AI-generated examples at issue here?

+ The author suggests that if deepfakes are to be used at all, "explicit consent from the person whose image or voice is being manipulated" is essential. How do you feel about this? Is this a sufficient safeguard? What additional protections might be needed?

+ Do you think that deepfake images, whether designed intentionally to deceive or for some other purpose, should be allowed at all? Should Christians and others generally abstain from them as a matter of course, or do they have a utility that should be appreciated?

CONNECTING TO OUR LIVES TODAY

Discuss:

+ What responsibility does the church have to model ethical AI use? How should it do this at the local, national, and global scales?

+ How can churches teach media literacy and digital fluency to their members? What should such training include?

+ The author suggests creating "scam-spotting training sessions" as part of safety training. What would you include in such a session?

+ Nathan recommends that churches create an AI policy collaboratively, with committed leaders. What would be involved in this process? Who should be included and how should it be run? What would the output look like?

+ "Bias, justice, privacy, and truth aren't optional, and they shouldn't be afterthoughts," says Nathan. Which of these is most urgent for your church to address? How are these issues interrelated?

CLOSING YOUR SESSION

Invite participants to share their own takeaways from this chapter. You might ask:

+ What ethical concern about AI did this chapter bring up that you hadn't fully considered before?

+ What boundary or policy does your church need to establish around AI use?

+ How can we as a faith community model authenticity and truth-telling in an age of deepfakes and misinformation?
+ What is one concrete step you or your church could take to build an "ethics engine" around AI use?

CLOSING PRAYER

God of justice and truth, we thank you for calling us to be people of integrity in all areas of life. In a world where deception spreads easily and truth is contested, help us to model authenticity, to speak truthfully, and to protect those vulnerable to manipulation and harm. Help us build churches and communities where privacy is honored, where marginalized voices can be heard, and where every person is treated with the dignity and respect you have granted them already. May we be faithful stewards of the power we wield through technology, using it always in service of your kingdom. Amen.

SESSION 5

The Church in the Age of Machines

SESSION GOALS

This session's reading, reflection, discussion, and prayer will help participants:

+ Understand and articulate what defines the church in light of digital innovation and technological change.
+ Explore the four marks of the church (evangelism, communion, discipleship, and sacrament) and how they can be authentically lived out with the use of digital platforms and AI-assisted tools.
+ Understand the Wesleyan Quadrilateral and its possibilities for use in discerning how to faithfully implement technology in ministry.
+ Envision how their own churches might intentionally incorporate technology while remaining grounded in their mission and the teachings of Christ.

BIBLICAL FOUNDATIONS

Now the eleven disciples went to Galilee, to the mountain to which Jesus had directed them. When they saw him, they worshiped him, but they doubted. And Jesus came and said to them, "All authority in heaven and on earth has been given to me. Go therefore and make disciples of all nations, baptizing them in the name of the Father and of the Son and of the Holy Spirit and teaching them to obey everything that I have commanded you. And remember, I am with you always, to the end of the age."

(Matthew 28:16-20)

Rid yourselves, therefore, of all malice and all guile, insincerity, envy, and all slander. Like newborn infants, long for the pure, spiritual milk, so that by it you may grow into salvation—if indeed you have tasted that the Lord is good.

Come to him, a living stone, though rejected by mortals yet chosen and precious in God's sight, and like living stones let yourselves be built into a spiritual house, to be a holy priesthood, to offer spiritual sacrifices acceptable to God through Jesus Christ. For it stands in scripture:

> *"See, I am laying in Zion a stone,*
> > *a cornerstone chosen and precious,*
> *and whoever believes in him will not be put to shame.". . .*

But you are a chosen people, a royal priesthood, a holy nation, God's own people, in order that you may proclaim the excellence of him who called you out of darkness into his marvelous light.

> *Once you were not a people,*
> > *but now you are God's people;*
> *once you had not received mercy,*
> > *but now you have received mercy.*

(1 Peter 2:1-6, 9-10)

BEFORE YOUR SESSION

- Carefully and prayerfully read this session's Biblical Foundations. Note words and phrases that attract your attention and think about them. Why did you find them of interest? Did they surprise you? Confuse you? Write down questions you have and try to answer them. You may want to consult trusted Bible commentaries.
- Carefully read chapter 5 of *God and the Machine*.
- You will need Bibles for in-person participants and/or screen slides prepared with Scripture texts for sharing (identify the translation used); for note-taking and brainstorming, you may want to have newsprint or a markerboard and markers; paper, pens or pencils.

STARTING YOUR SESSION

Invite participants to share about the use of technology in the church.

- In your time being Christian and/or part of a church community, what new technologies have developed? How have any of these changed your experience of worship or church life? What positives and negatives have you seen from these new technologies?
- Some examples are television, email, the internet and websites, projector screens in worship, electronic newsletters, cellular phones, online videos of church services, and even computer programs for accounting, publishing, and other church functions.

OPENING PRAYER

God, be with us as we gather here to explore what it means to be the church today. Each day and age brings its own challenges, and like so many Christians before us, we are called to reimagine what church can be for the present and for the future. Open our minds to new possibilities while helping us to stay true to our commitments and rooted in our traditions. Allow us to step into the future with boldness and humility, drawing the circle ever wider so that new generations may know your name and your love. Amen.

DEFINING WHAT MAKES CHURCH *CHURCH*

Discuss:

+ Nathan notes that churches have often answered the question of their ecclesiology "decades (if not centuries) ago and haven't taken the time to review it." Do you feel this is true for your church or denomination or the global church as a whole? How well does the church at these different levels do at adapting itself to the cultural, social, and historical context?

+ How much should churches be doing to adapt to these changing circumstances? What are the risks and benefits of changing the model of how churches operate?

+ Nathan reflects on the early church in Acts and John Wesley's model of small groups. What do these historical models tell us about the essential nature of church and Methodist churches in particular?

- The author notes that church planters must not only have vision for the church moving forward but also translate what is happening to those outside looking in. Why is this translation important?
- How does Nathan distinguish between a church and "just a club or a community"? What makes the difference for him? How would you explain the difference between these social groups?

THE CHURCH REACHES OUT

Discuss:

- Nathan argues that the church cannot always remain the same and must change and grow. How does this align with, or challenge, your understanding of the church's purpose?
- What are the advantages and potential pitfalls of using digital platforms for evangelism? How can these concerns be mitigated?
- Nathan shares that people in nerdy communities naturally evangelize their interests. How might this model of organic enthusiasm apply to faith communities?
- Sermons at Checkpoint Church often involve references to gaming, internet culture, and other things that may be particularly relevant to its congregants. How does meeting people where they are in terms of their interests and online spaces align with the Great Commission and the general demand for evangelism in Christianity?
- What role might AI play in amplifying evangelistic efforts while remaining faithful to the gospel message?

THE CHURCH BUILDS WITHIN

Discuss:

+ Why is gathering together essential to being church? What does Matthew 18:20 suggest about Christ's presence in community?

+ Hebrews 10:24 speaks of spurring one another on to love and good deeds and encouraging one another. How do digital gatherings accomplish this? What might be lost or gained?

+ This section addresses the argument that digital church cannot be "real" because participants are not physically embodied together. Do you find his argument convincing? What are your thoughts on this topic? What is the value and potential issues with such new models of church?

+ The author notes that participants in his digital church describe it as "an embodied gathering that many call their church." What makes an online gathering "embodied"?

+ What practices or structures might help a digital congregation truly function as a gathered community rather than isolated individuals? More generally, how can digital communities incorporate practices that grow and deepen relationships and communal well-being?

THE CHURCH GROWS PEOPLE

Discuss:

+ Nathan writes: "The church is defined by a process of holiness that is ongoing." How does this understanding of the church differ from other community organizations?

- First Peter 2:9 speaks of being called "out of darkness into his marvelous light." What does Nathan mean when he says discipleship is about being on a path "further into that marvelous light"?
- Nathan describes developing a discipleship pathway: evangelism →community→discipleship→sacrament→stewardship. Why is this sequence important? What would happen if steps were skipped or reordered?
- The author notes that Checkpoint's "rules" are adapted from John Wesley's General Rules: "do good, do no harm, and strive to grow." How do these simple rules capture the essence of Christian discipleship?
- What resources or structures help people move deeper in their faith journey? How might AI assist in this process without replacing human relationships?
- What does it mean to join a church and to be "on a path of deeper discipleship"? How is this different from simply joining a community organization?

THE CHURCH IS SET APART

Discuss:

- What makes the sacraments fundamentally different from other community practices?
- Nathan states, "We are a living organism, engaged in the past tradition and still today, growing ourselves into the ongoing evolution of what the early church instituted." What does he mean by this understanding of sacramental practice?
- Nathan notes that Checkpoint practices Communion weekly online and has developed an app that allows members to press

a button to indicate their presence in the body of Christ and to create communal atmosphere. What is your reaction to this? Would you want to be part of a community like the one described here?

+ Although Checkpoint has not yet practiced baptism online, the author notes that others have conducted baptisms over Zoom and other platforms. What do you think of this practice? What are the considerations for administering sacraments digitally?

+ If the church is fundamentally about "something holy going on," how do we ensure that digital practices preserve this holy character?

AND ALSO ONLINE

Discuss:

+ Nathan provides concrete examples of how all four marks of the church (evangelism, communion, discipleship, sacrament) are practiced at Checkpoint online. Which of these practices surprises you most? Which seems most challenging to imagine?

+ How might your own church's practices be enhanced or expanded through digital tools while remaining faithful to your self-understanding and mission?

BUT WHAT ABOUT AI?

Discuss:

+ Nathan notes that AI determines algorithms for evangelistic reach, fuels Discord bots, and helps discipleship content find audiences. How might AI already be shaping your church's work, even if it is not explicitly used or discussed?

+ Have you encountered the Wesleyan Quadrilateral before?
  Have you found it useful for thinking through dilemmas and
  difficult issues? What aspects of it have been helpful (or not)?

+ This section applies the Quadrilateral to a specific question:
  Should AI provide pastoral counseling? Walk through the
  author's reasoning using each aspect. Do you agree with his
  conclusion?

+ How might the Quadrilateral help your church discern other
  questions about AI use?

CONNECTING TO OUR LIVES TODAY

Discuss:

+ What is your church's current ecclesiology? Can you articulate it
  clearly? When was it last examined?

+ Of the four marks of the church (evangelism, communion,
  discipleship, sacrament), which does your church emphasize
  most? Which might be neglected?

+ How might digital technology help your church live out each of
  these marks more fully?

+ What concerns do you have about implementing digital
  practices in your church community?

+ Nathan writes that technology should never drive the church—
  the church should be in the driver's seat. How can your church
  maintain this priority?

+ Is there a specific technology decision your church needs to
  make? How might the Wesleyan Quadrilateral help guide that
  decision?

CLOSING YOUR SESSION

Discuss the following questions:

+ Considering some of the ideas presented in the book and during this discussion, for you, what defines the church? What are its most important characteristic marks?
+ How does your ideal of church at times diverge from the reality?
+ What is one way your church could use technology more intentionally?

CLOSING PRAYER

God, you have made us called to others. We are social beings who have an inborn desire to be with others. We thank you for the gift of community— whether gathered in person or through digital connections. We thank you for this gathering today, for our church community, for our families and friends, and any others that allow us to gather in your name. We are reminded continually that no technology, no machine can replace these human relationships. In your name we pray. Amen.

SESSION 6

Human-Forward Thinking

SESSION GOALS

This session's reading, reflection, discussion, and prayer will help participants:

+ Understand what it means to be embodied in digital spaces.
+ Develop a human-forward approach to AI implementation that prioritizes human agency, flourishing, and embodied presence over technological efficiency.
+ Recognize the importance of trust, grace, and right judgment in responding to AI adoption and misuse.
+ Envision how the church can shape the narrative around AI and metaverse technologies by modeling faithful, intentional, and justice-oriented practices.

BIBLICAL FOUNDATIONS

Or do you not know that your body is a temple of the Holy Spirit within you, which you have from God, and that you are not your own? For you were bought with a price; therefore glorify God in your body.

(1 Corinthians 6:19-20)

When I look at your heavens, the work of your fingers,
the moon and the stars that you have established;
what are humans that you are mindful of them,
mortals that you care for them?

Yet you have made them a little lower than God
and crowned them with glory and honor.
You have given them dominion over the works of your hands;
you have put all things under their feet,
all sheep and oxen,
and also the beasts of the field,
the birds of the air, and the fish of the sea,
whatever passes along the paths of the seas.

(Psalm 8:3-8)

BEFORE YOUR SESSION

+ Carefully and prayerfully read this session's Biblical Foundations. Note words and phrases that attract your attention and think about them. Why did you find them of interest? Did they surprise you? Confuse you? Write down questions you have and try to answer them. You may want to consult trusted Bible commentaries.
+ Carefully read chapter 6 of *God and the Machine*.
+ You will need Bibles for in-person participants and/or screen slides prepared with Scripture texts for sharing (identify the translation used); for note-taking and brainstorming, you may

want to have newsprint or a markerboard and markers; paper, pens or pencils.

STARTING YOUR SESSION

Welcome participants. Ask them to think about a time they felt genuinely connected to another person through a digital medium (social media, message boards, a text or call, etc.). Invite a few volunteers to share about that experience. What made it feel genuine and connected? How did the digital experience spill over into the rest of your life?

OPENING PRAYER

God of flesh and spirit, you created us as embodied beings who are called to live in community with one another. Help us to see technology not as a replacement for human presence but as a means to extend and amplify our capacity to love and serve one another. May we never forget that we are called to be the body of Christ, a loving community of people who today incarnate your Son through the power of the Spirit. Amen.

GHOST IN THE MACHINE: UNDERSTANDING THE METAPHOR

Discuss:

+ What does the author mean by "ghost in the machine"? Why is this phrase significant for understanding how people perceive AI?
+ Nathan notes that science fiction has long explored questions about the distinction between mind and body, and human and machine. How might these fictional scenarios shape how we

think about AI today? What examples have influenced how you think about these issues?

+ The author mentions that people form parasocial relationships with AI, treating it like a therapist or a friend. Why do you think people are drawn to do this? Have you ever engaged with an AI or other form of technology in this way?

+ Is the empathy expressed by AI "real"? What does it mean to be "real" (or genuine or sincere) in this context?

+ The chapter opens with tension between despair and responsibility. Why does the author argue that the opposite of despair about AI isn't hope but responsibility? What is the importance of responsibility here? What role does hope have in how we think about AI and its use?

WHOSE BODY IS IT ANYWAY?

Discuss:

+ Nathan notes that Genesis emphasizes the body as vital to human life. Are there other biblical passages or ideas that seem to go against this stress on embodiment? How do you think about embodiment and its importance to faith and relation to topics like the afterlife and resurrection?

+ Paul writes in 1 Corinthians 15 about spiritual bodies being raised in glory. Nathan asks, "Is this metaphorical or literal? Is the transformation happening on this side of our lives or after an earthly demise?" How do you understand statements like we find here in Paul?

+ Do you agree with the author that it is important to understand our digital presence as embodied in a significant way? Have you thought about digital life in these terms before?

* How do you feel in general about the gravity and importance of relationships formed online? Are they fundamentally different from in-person relationships?

* "I send a piece of myself, mediated through wires and screens, bits and bytes," writes Nathan. What does this mean? When you communicate digitally, do you ever envision that you are sending a piece of yourself? How might it change things to think in this way?

THE PHYSICAL COST OF DIGITAL CONNECTION

Discuss:

* Nathan acknowledges the darker side of embodied digital life, which can include physical strain, anxiety, stress, and shame from online interactions. Have you experienced these? How might recognizing them change our thinking about digital connection?

* He also argues against simply telling people to get out of the house and reduce their use of digital services. Why might this be an inadequate response?

* Have you ever struggled with being too online or using a particular app or service too frequently? What strategies worked to help with this issue?

* How might churches support healthy digital practices and media literacy rather than assuming "everyone is an addict who cannot regulate"?

STOP BEFORE IT STARTS

Discuss:

+ The author contrasts human-forward with technology-forward approaches, using Grammarly as an example of the former, a sort of augmentation to human activity. What would be a technology-forward example? Does this distinction seem important to you?

+ If you read a book, recited a prayer, or heard a sermon that you enjoyed and later found out was AI-generated, would this change how you feel about it? What would shift, if anything? How does this change with different types of media?

+ Nathan raises the ecological cost of AI, particularly data centers that consume vast amounts of water and energy. Should environmental concerns factor into our decisions about AI use? How?

+ The author emphasizes that "we should be signaling to the algorithm what is a healthy use of these models." What does this mean? How can our individual usage shape AI's development?

+ Nathan notes he's very much aware of his daughters watching him use (or not use) AI. Why might modeling healthy boundaries matter here? How have you modeled making good decisions around technology to others, especially children or others who might look up to you?

THE VALUE OF TRUST

Discuss:

+ The author expresses empathy with students facing pressure and suspicion around AI use. He recalls earlier panic about

Wikipedia and how students adapted by using it differently. Does this historical parallel help us think about current AI concerns? Is there something different in these two scenarios?

+ Nathan offers critiques of those who reject any use of AI and withdraw support from those who use it. How might this "never AI" attitude present problems for the church?

+ Wesleyan thought emphasizes social holiness, which involves social trust. Why might division around technology threaten social holiness? How can we rebuild trust here?

A METAVERSAL TRUTH

Discuss:

+ Nathan defines the metaverse as "an interconnected universe of digital spaces" where people interact through digital environments and avatars. Have you ever participated in such spaces? What are their possibilities and dangers?

+ This section distinguishes between obvious metaverse interactions (VR headsets) and less obvious ones (Discord servers, emoji reactions, DMs). Is it helpful to see all of these as metaversal in a meaningful way? What ways of thinking and understanding might the concept of metaverse open up for you?

+ The author predicts that "our metaverse future looks less like VR headsets and full immersion and more like a Discord server . . . a neo-monastic society." What do you make of this possibility? What of the use of the term *neo-monastic* here?

+ Nathan emphasizes that AI is already woven into metaverse technology in social media algorithms, video games, and virtual reality. If the metaverse is part of the future, what responsibility does the church have to engage with it?

+ "If the church wishes to remain connected to the lives of our communities in the future, we must be aware of what it means to bring Christ to the metaverse." What would this look like?

MORE THAN A GHOST

Discuss:

+ Nathan writes: "God is not the machine, nor is the machine a god." Why is this distinction important? What errors might result from failing to maintain this boundary?

+ The author argues: "The church should be less interested in seeing some kind of divine inspiration from code and numbers . . . and more interested in how God uses technology at all." What's the difference?

+ Nathan states: "It can likely research more effectively, schedule better, and write faster—but it cannot be better neighbors. It cannot be the embodied people online." What can AI never do? What can it not replace? Do you have a different, more restrictive, or more expansive understanding of its capabilities than the author?

+ Have you found it helpful or clarifying to have love of God and neighbor as driving concerns when discussing and thinking about AI? What other key concerns would you want included here, perhaps ones not raised by the author?

CONNECTING TO OUR LIVES TODAY

Discuss:

+ What does "human-forward" thinking look like in your own use of technology? Can you think of ways you use AI or other tools as augmentation versus replacement?

- How might your church adopt a more intentional, human-forward approach to technology? What would need to change?
- Nathan emphasizes trust and grace in responding to AI misuse. How does this differ from the current cultural approach in education and society? Why should the church model a different way?
- What role might your church play in shaping how communities understand and use AI? How could you model healthy boundaries and practices?
- What is one ecological or social concern about AI that your church should address?

CLOSING YOUR SESSION

This is a good time to review some of the things you have talked about throughout the sessions and reflect on the most important or meaningful ideas that have come up.

- What are the most surprising or important things you have learned about AI and how we should confront it as Christians?
- Have your views changed or shifted at all since we began this group?
- What is one commitment you want to make about how you use technology going forward?
- What do you think the church and society more broadly should do to confront the potentially problematic aspects of AI? What rules, guidelines, and guardrails should be in place?

CLOSING PRAYER

God, we thank you for our time together in this group. We thank you for the connections made, the information learned, and the discussions shared.

As we leave here today, help us be mindful of what we have learned as we seek to apply it in our lives, each in our own way. Help us and our church use the tools available to us in ethical ways that place people and God at the center. And remind us continually that in spite of the ever-forward march of innovation and the changing shape of the world around us, you are our rock—steadfast and faithful to the end of time. Amen.

www.ingramcontent.com/pod-product-compliance
Lightning Source LLC
LaVergne TN
LVHW030830291225
828363LV00010B/29